African
Fables

African Fables

That teach about God

Compiled by Eudene Keidel

Illustrated by Kathy Bartel

HERALD PRESS
Scottdale, Pennsylvania
Kitchener, Ontario

The Bible verses in this book are taken from *The Living Bible, Paraphrased* (Wheaton: Tyndale House Publishers, 1971) and are used by permission.

AFRICAN FABLES
Copyright © 1978 by Herald Press, Scottdale, Pa. 15683
    Published simultaneously in Canada by Herald Press,
    Kitchener, Ont. N2G 4M5
Library of Congress Catalog Card Number: 77-15709
International Standard Book Number: 0-8361-1842-1
Printed in the United States of America

10 9 8 7 6 5 4 3

Contents

(Including Topic and Reading Time in Minutes)

Preface

During our four terms of missionary service in Zaire, I have often heard Africans tell stories drawn from their folklore. I've heard pastors use them from the pulpit to teach spiritual lessons; I've listened to older village people relate them around the fire at night; I've read some from their literature.

I have told these stories to children in many places and now share some of them with you here. They show something of the richness of African culture, from which we could learn much. Enjoy them, and tell them to your children again and again.

Eudene Keidel
Fort Wayne, Indiana

1

Why the Turtle Has a
Mottled Shell

MR. TURTLE lived on the sandbank by the river. One day as he sunned himself there he began feeling sorry for himself. Nobody paid attention to him; he was so lonely. He was hungry too. He hadn't eaten a good meal for so long that his body rattled in his shell. How good it would be to have some friends! How he would enjoy some nice fresh worms!

Then he began listening to the birds in the branches of the tree above him. They were very excited. What were they saying? A big party?

He stretched his head out from under his shell and called up to them, "Did you say you are going to a party?"

"Yes," they replied. "The King of the Sky is having a party; he is inviting all the birds to come."

"May I go too?" asked the turtle.

"The last time you came to our party you ruined it for us. No, you may not go."

"I'll be good this time," promised the turtle. "Please let me go. I'll not spoil the party."

The turtle begged and begged until finally the birds said, "All right, you may go with us. But the party is up in the sky. How are you going to get there? You can't fly."

"If each of you gave me two big feathers, I think I could," he replied.

Finally the day arrived for the party. They gathered at the taking-off place, and each bird gave Mr. Turtle two feathers. The birds took off. Mr. Turtle held the feathers in his claws tightly and waved them up and down real hard. His body began to lift up, and sure enough, he started to fly!

Down below he saw his sandbank and the village where people lived. He was so excited he tingled all over with happiness. But it wasn't long until he began feeling his old meaness again. Then he said to the birds, "Did you know that when you go to a party like this you should give yourself a new name? People always do."

"No, we didn't know that," said the birds. They talked about it and decided that the turtle had been in the world so much longer than any of them that he was probably right. So each of them thought of a new name.

"What name are going to give yourself?" they asked the turtle.

"My name will be 'You All.' "

The birds thought You All was a funny name, but they didn't say anything.

Finally they all arrived at the place of the King of the Sky. The King was so happy to see them. He was especially happy to see Mr. Turtle. The King thought Mr. Turtle was the funniest bird he had ever seen. He decided to give Mr. Turtle the seat of honor at the head of the table.

Mr. Turtle sat in his big chair and looked over the table. It was covered with a pretty white cloth and was just loaded with things birds and turtles like to eat. There was a big bowl of wiggly worms, and a bowl of little black insects, and a bowl of tender little green leaves, and a bowl of brown seeds. Mr. Turtle was so excited he could hardly wait. His mouth watered until it was full. He swallowed and asked Mr. King of the Sky, "Excuse me, sir. For whom did you prepare this wonderful feast?"

"I made it for you all," the King replied.

Mr. Turtle turned to the birds and said, "Did you hear that? He prepared the feast for You All. That's my name. Now you wait until I'm through."

Mr. Turtle ate and ate. He ate all the bugs and worms, most of the green leaves, and some of the seeds. The birds sat and watched. They became more and more angry.

Finally Mr. Turtle's tummy was so full it felt like it would burst his shell. Then he sat back and told the birds they could eat. The birds looked at the scraps on the tablecloth and the messy bowls, and were so angry they decided to go home. As each bird left, he walked past Mr. Turtle and took his two feathers. Mr. Turtle began to worry. Finally, only Mr. Parrot's feathers were left. When Mr. Parrot came by, Mr. Turtle asked him, "Are you going to take my last two feathers? How am I going to get home?"

"That's your problem," replied the parrot taking his feathers. "You ruined our party. Find your own way home."

"Then, please, Mr. Parrot, take a message to my wife."

"What do you want me to tell your wife?"

"Tell her to put all our soft things out in the yard—our mattresses and pillows and rugs. Then when I fall it won't hurt me so much."

Mr. Parrot went to Mrs. Turtle. He said to her, "Mr. Turtle said to tell you to put all your hard things out in the yard."

Mrs. Turtle didn't understand this strange order, but she always tried to obey her husband. So she put all the rakes and hoes and chairs and buckets and Mr. Turtle's bicycle out in the yard, and went into the house to wait.

Mr. Turtle was watching from up in the sky. But because he was nearsighted, he could not tell for sure what she was doing. When it looked like she was done, he took a big breath, let go, and came tumbling down. When he got close enough to see, he realized that she had put all the hard things in the yard, but he couldn't stop. He landed kerplunk in the middle of them.

Mrs. Turtle heard the crash and came rushing out to see what had happened. She found him lying there moaning, his shell all broken into pieces. Mrs. Turtle called the turtle doctor, and he patched up Mr. Turtle's shell the best he could. That's why you see Mr. Turtle's back like it is. Those are all the broken pieces grown back together again.

Do you like someone who always wants the largest apple or the biggest piece of candy? No, I don't think any of us like selfish people. The Bible says we are to be kind one to another. But when someone always wants his own way no matter what, that's not being kind. That's being selfish. And selfish people will always lose their friends, as Mr. Turtle did.

So today let's see who we are going to be like— Mr. Turtle who was greedy and selfish, or the King in the Sky who wanted to be kind.

2

Bad Dinners

MR. LEOPARD had often looked hungrily at the monkeys and wondered how he could catch them. One day he thought to himself, "I'll make a big feast and invite the monkeys to come. Then I can catch them for myself." So he set a date and invited them.

Now the monkeys had a wise sentry who guarded them while they played. He told them, "Don't trust the leopard. He's probably up to one of his mean tricks. All of you go to the feast. I'll hide in a tree nearby and guard you. If the leopard tries to do something bad, I'll warn you."

The feast day came and all the monkeys except the wise old sentry gathered at Mr. Leopard's house. The table was all set outside, but there was no food on it. When the monkeys arrived Mr. Leopard said to them, "It's nice to see all of you. I'll get the food and we can eat."

Then the leopard went around to the back side of his hut. The sentry was watching him closely. Instead of getting food, he was fixing a big bag to put the monkeys in. The sentry shouted a warning, and all the monkeys scampered up into the trees again.

When the leopard came back to the table he called and called, but the monkeys refused to come down.

Not many days later the monkeys invited the leopard to their own feast in the forest. They had spread lots of food on the leaves of the forest floor. The leopard came happily. When he arrived he saw the table loaded with good things to eat. When the monkeys gave the word to begin the meal, the leopard greedily jumped into the center of the table, and WHOOoosh, down he went into the ground, cloth and all. What Mr. Leopard didn't know was that the table was really a trap for him. Underneath the monkeys had dug a big, deep hole. When he fell into the hole, he couldn't jump out. He called and called for the monkeys to help him, but they only danced around the hole and made fun of him.

Sometimes people pretend they are friends, but really they are just trying to trick each other. Some people say they are our friends, but when we get into trouble, they desert us. Some of them may even make fun of us. Real friends help one another and care for each other. This is the way it should be between us and our friends.

The Bible says a real friend will stick closer than a brother. (Proverbs 18:24). Jesus wants to be such a Friend to each one of us. He is a Friend who will always love us. Do you know Him as your own personal Friend?

3

The Crow Who Wouldn't Pay His Debt

MR. CROW was making a garden big enough to feed himself and his two wives. Digging up the black soil with his little beak was hard work. One day he watched Mr. Hornbill fly overhead.

"Oh, Mr. Hornbill, come here," cried the crow. "I think you can help me."

The hornbill circled around and landed on a dead stump near Mr. Crow.

"I have to dig up this garden before the rains start, but I find the work very tiring. You have a big beak. Could I hire you to plow it for me? I'll pay you well."

"Fine," said Mr. Hornbill.

The hornbill plowed up the whole garden in two days. Then he came to Mr. Crow's house to get his pay.

"I didn't know you were such a good worker," the crow said. "You finished so soon that I'm not prepared to pay you yet. Come back in a few days."

After a few days the hornbill returned. But he found only the wives at home. "Mr. Crow went

18

away to get your pay, and hasn't returned yet," they said.

After a week the hornbill came back. "Mr. Crow still hasn't returned," the wives said.

Mr. Hornbill came back again and again, and always was given the same story. Finally he became angry and told the wives, "If Mr. Crow doesn't bring me my money soon, I'm going to tell Judge Owl. He'll call your husband to court and make him pay." Angry and sad, he went on his way home.

Along the path he met a poor old widow bird returning from the stream.

"Why do you have such a long, long face today?" she asked him.

"Because I've come to Mr. Crow's house ten times to get my money, and he won't pay me."

"Oh, are you the one Mr. Crow is laughing at? My hut is on the backside of the village near the forest. Mr. Crow has made himself a place to hide in a palm tree there. When the noise of your wings tells him that you are on the way, he flies to the palm tree to hide. He dances and sings songs mocking you, while you sit at his house waiting for him. If you spread tar on the limb where he sits, you would soon put an end to his foolishness."

That night, when everybody was asleep, the hornbill brought tar, found the crow's hiding place, and rubbed tar on the limb. The next day he took an empty basket with a lid on it and went to Mr. Crow's house.

"He hasn't returned yet," the wives said. "We just can't understand why it is taking him so long."

Mr. Hornbill flew to the palm tree and found Mr. Crow stuck to the limb. He pulled out his wing feathers so he couldn't fly, put him into the basket, tied it shut, and took him home. He kept Mr. Crow in his basket-prison until his wives came with money to pay him for his work.

We are not to do things which stir up trouble with our friends and neighbors. The Bible says, "Stop being mean. ... Instead, be kind to each other, tenderhearted, forgiving one another" (Ephesians 4:31, 32). "Don't quarrel with anyone. Be at peace with everyone, just as much as possible" (Romans 12:18).

How a Lizard Got Everybody into Trouble

A TURTLE, a lizard who couldn't hear very well, and a snail all lived together in one place. For a while they enjoyed living together.

Then one day the turtle decided that he would see what was out in the forest. As he wandered through the bushes he came to a big tree with a hole at the bottom. He said to himself, "When this tree has fruit on it, it will be a good place to live. This shall be my home." So he crawled into the hole and made himself comfortable.

One day the lizard said, "I wonder what has happened to Friend Turtle?" He decided he would go look for him in the forest. He hunted for a long time, and finally found him by the tree. He said, "This is a nice place to live. I will stay here by you."

"No," said the turtle. "You go find someplace else to live."

But the lizard had trouble hearing the turtle's words. He climbed up the trunk, onto a branch, found a shady place, and stayed.

Not many days later the snail wondered what

had become of his two friends. He decided to go look for them. He hunted and hunted and finally found the turtle. Then he climbed up the tree and found the lizard.

He said to the lizard, "I would like to live here too."

The lizard said, "You cannot live close to me. Go find another place."

Now there was a vine which climbed from the ground up into the tree branches. The snail climbed about half way down the vine, fastened himself to a leaf, and stayed.

One day the fruit on the tree became ripe. Many monkeys and birds of the forest came to eat it. They began scolding each other and made a lot of noise. The turtle living at the bottom of the tree called to the snail, "Friend Snail, call Friend Lizard to tell the birds and monkeys to be quiet. If you fail, death will catch all of us."

The snail called out one time, "Friend Lizard, tell the birds and monkeys to stop making so much noise. If you fail, death will catch all of us." Then he went back inside his cozy shell. But the lizard couldn't hear well, and he didn't bother to ask the snail what he had said.

A hunter came into the forest. He heard the noise in the tree and came to see what it was all about. He had never seen so many birds in one tree. He thought, "Today I have good luck." He shot an arrow into the tree, and down came two birds. They hit the lizard and knocked it down too.

The hunter shot again, and down came a monkey.

When the monkey fell, he hit the vine and knocked down the snail. The hunter put them all into his bag. Finally he saw the turtle. He picked him up and put him into the bag too.

On the way back to the village, the turtle was crying over their bad luck, and said to his friend the lizard, "See what happened? Now we're all in the same trouble. I told you that if you failed, death would catch all of us. But you didn't think what I said was important, and refused to pay attention."

That's the way it is in life. Adam disobeyed God, and so sin and death came into the world. If he had always obeyed God, he wouldn't have gotten everybody into trouble.

People act like they don't hear the truth. They just keep living their lives all to themselves. They don't want to believe that unless they heed God's words, they will die eternally.

But the Bible says that while one man brought sin into the world, another Man came and brought life into the world (Romans 5:12-21). This Man is Jesus Christ. Are you paying attention to God's warning? Are you following Jesus?

5

Mr. Rat Tricks a
Tricky Lion

THE RAT and the lion had been friends for a long
time. The rat always tried to be kind to Mr. Lion,
even when Mr. Lion treated him badly.

Mr. Lion decided that he would trick Mr. Rat and
catch him. After thinking about it a long time, one
day he told his wife, "Wife Lion, I know what I'll
do. You send Mr. Rat word that I'm very sick, and it
doesn't look like I'll recover. I have some important
final words to give him. Then he'll come and I can
catch him."

So Mrs. Lion sent word to Mr. Rat that his friend
Mr. Lion was very ill, and that he should come as
soon as possible so that Mr. Lion could give him his
parting words.

When Mr. Rat received the message he thought
to himself, "Mr. Lion is trying to trick me." So he
paid no attention to it.

This made Mr. Lion very angry. Now he was de-
termined to catch Mr. Rat and eat him up. One day
he said to his wife, "I know what I'll do. Send Mr.
Rat word that I have died. He will come and mourn

my death because we have always been friends."

Mrs. Lion sent Mr. Rat the message. Then Mr. Lion lay down on his mat with his knife beside him, and Mrs. Lion covered him with a blanket. They waited for Mr. Rat to come.

When Mr. Rat received the message he said to himself, "I don't want to offend Friend Lion, but I think he's trying to fool me. I'll go and test him." Then he headed for Mr. Lion's house.

When he was some distance away he began to wail and mourn. "Oh, Friend Lion, why did you die? My friend, my friend, what will I do without you?"

Mrs. Lion met him in the path and said, "Why didn't you come when my husband was ill? He had words to leave with you."

"There were other important things which kept me home. But I'm here now," answered the rat.

"You were such a good friend of Mr. Lion. You must come here and sit in the chief mourner's chair close to my husband's head."

"Before I take my place in the chair, let me say that I'm terribly sorry about Mr. Lion's death," the rat said comfortingly. "I'll need to call all the jungle animals to come help me bury him properly."

"But first sit in the chair. Your mourning will make me feel better," said Mrs. Lion.

"In our tribe we never bury a friend without knowing for sure that he's dead. How cruel it would be to bury my friend and your husband if he should still have life in him. I'll try two things to make sure he is dead. Then I'll sit in the chair and mourn for him."

Mr. Lion was listening carefully. He certainly didn't want the other animals to come and bury him alive. Neither did he want them to know about his tricking Mr. Rat. Still, he wanted to pass the test so that Mr. Rat would come close to him. He didn't know what to do.

Mr. Rat stood on the front side of Mr. Lion and said in a loud voice, "Friend Lion, if you're really dead, raise you right hand high."

Mr. Lion's arm shot up high.

Mr. Rat smiled to himself. He returned to Mr. Lion's back side so that he was between Mr. Lion and the burrow in the ground which was his home.

Then he called out again, "Oh, Friend Lion, if you're really dead, you'll shake all over."

At that Mr. Lion began shaking all over under the blanket. Suddenly he realized how the rat was tricking him. He leaped up, grabbed his knife, and lunged toward Mr. Rat. But the rat was too quick for him, and ran as fast as he could go to his burrow. He crawled into it and sat down to rest. He was so out of breath he didn't realize that he hadn't pulled his tail into the hole. Suddenly Mr. Lion pounced on Mr. Rat's tail with his big paw.

Mr. Rat called out, "Mr. Lion, why are you trying to hold onto that little old tree root?" The lion lifted his paw a little bit to look at it, and the rat pulled his tail to safety. Mr. Lion roared with anger because he had been outwitted by a little rat.

The Bible tells us that Satan is wandering around like a roaring lion ready to tear us apart (1 Peter 5:8). He's trying to deceive us. He wants to destroy us. He'll do anything he can to make us sin and do what is wrong. We should never make friends with him. We should be alert in our minds and not let him trick us.

The best way to defeat the devil is to give our hearts to Jesus and to try in every way to please Him. The Bible says, "Resist the devil and he will flee from you" (James 4:7).

6

Where Can You Find a Piece of the Wind?

A VILLAGE man was very proud of his son. He had waited a long time for a little boy. When the baby was finally born he promised himself that he would be a faithful father and teach the lad all the wisdom he needed to avoid life's problems.

Mooka, the little boy, grew rapidly and was the joy of his father's heart.

Then came the day for him to begin to learn the lessons of life. Father called him and said, "Mooka, I want you to grow up to be wise and good."

The boy said, "Daddy, I am wise and good. I have been good from the day I was born."

"My boy," the father replied, "the only person Who could honestly say that was God's Son."

"I'm not God's Son," Mooka said. "But we young people these days get wise faster than you old folks do. I don't need your wisdom."

The father was very disappointed. "Mooka," he said, "who has taught you such pride and disrespect? Do you mean that you are more able to answer the difficult questions of life than your father? You'll have to prove yourself before I'll accept talk like that."

Mooka became a young man. He went to his father and said, "I want to find the girl who will be my wife."

"You're old enough to know what you want," the father said. "Go find her."

Mooka found a pretty girl whom he liked very much. He went to her father who was a wise old village elder.

"I'd like to marry you daughter," Mooka said. "How much bride price are you asking for her?"

"It would be all right if her husband were rich," replied the old man, "but it's more important that he be wise. So I'm not asking for money. All I'm asking for is a piece of the wind."

Mooka didn't know what to answer the old man, so he went home to his father.

"I've found the girl I would like to marry," he said. "She's the daughter of an old village elder."

"Fine," replied Father. "What's he asking for bride price?"

"He says he doesn't want money. All he wants is a piece of the wind."

"You've always boasted about how wise you are. Put your knife into your belt and take your hunting bag and go after it."

Mooka didn't know how to answer. He got his knife and hunting bag and went into the forest to think over his problem. Maybe he should forget about this girl, and find another one with an easier bride price. But he loved her so much he was sure he would never really be happy with a different one. Still it was silly for him to try to cut off a piece of the wind and keep it inside his hunting bag. Who in the world could do something like that? Was his father really wise enough to answer this riddle? He went back to his house.

"Father, solving this problem is too hard for me. Please help me if you can."

"Mooka," his father reminded him, "I told you to search for wisdom. Now you have failed. Come. Let's go to the house of the girl's father."

They arrived at the house, said hello, shook

hands, and sat down. Then Father asked the elder, "Friend, please give me a cup of drinking water." Taking the cup from the man's hand, he studied the water quietly and then said, "But friend, are you giving your guest water which has not been ground and sifted?"

"Why, where do they every grind and sift water?" asked the old man.

"The same place where they catch pieces of the wind," Father said.

"I offered my daughter to the one who could answer that riddle to test his wisdom," the old man said. "You have answered it wisely. I will be glad for your son to marry my daughter."

We may sometimes feel that our parents aren't up-to-date and that we know best. But we must remember that they have had many more lessons in life than we, and unless we listen to what they are trying to tell us, we may be put to shame like foolish Mooka.

The Bible says, "Honor your father and mother, that you may have a long, good life in the land the Lord your God will give you" (Exodus 20:12). "A wise youth accepts his father's rebuke. . . . Sad [is] the mother of a rebel" (Proverbs 13:1, 10:1).

7

The Frog's Strange Rules
About Dinner

A MONKEY and a frog often met each other on the path in the forest. The frog decided they should learn to know each other better. He would prepare a special dinner called a "friendship meal" and ask the monkey over to eat with him. That would seal their friendship forever.

The next day the frog saw his friend the monkey and said to him, "Tomorrow I am fixing a friendship meal for you and me to 'eat friendship' together. Will you come?"

"I surely will," replied the monkey. "What time?"

"When the sun is starting to go to bed, you be there."

The monkey could hardly wait until the sun started to go down so that he could go eat with his friend the frog.

When the monkey arrived at the frog's house he saw a big feast indeed. The frog had killed a goat and two chickens, and had cooked a delicious meal. The monkey could hardly wait to eat.

For the first time, the frog noticed that the

monkey had black hands. The frog was not used to eating food with hands like that. *How ugly!* he thought. So he said, "Before we eat, we must wash our hands white."

They went to the river together to wash and scrub their hands. The frog's hands were soon white. The monkey scrubbed and scrubbed, but his hands would not turn white. He scrubbed them with sand. He rubbed them onto a stone. He scrubbed until some of the hair and skin came off.

The frog said to him, "I've fixed a big feast for you and now you can't eat it because your hands are black. Do I have to eat my feast with somebody who has dirty hands?"

This made the monkey angry and he went home. The frog could eat the feast by himself if that's the way he felt.

After the monkey got home he planned a way to get even with the frog. He fixed a grand feast and sent the frog an invitation. When the frog arrived he found that the monkey had placed all the food on a big branch high in a tree.

The frog frowned and said to the monkey, "Friend Monkey, I cannot climb a tree."

"Oh, that's all right. I'll help you," replied the monkey. So he boosted the frog up the trunk and into the tree.

The frog was terribly frightened to be up so high, but he didn't want the monkey to know it. Then the monkey said, "Whoever comes to my feast must sit up straight like I do."

The frog didn't know what to do. Finally he tried

real hard to sit up straight on his hind feet like the monkey, but he lost his balance and fell kerplunk to the ground. He picked himself up, dusted himself off, and went home hungry and ashamed.

We shouldn't make fun of other people who are different from us. God made us as we are, and all of us are worth the same in His sight.

The Bible says that God made of one blood all the races of mankind (Acts 17:26). If God has made us that way, who are we to think somebody should have been made a different way?

8

Little Feather-Picking Sparrows

MOTHER SPARROW had built herself a nest in the fork of a tree out on the plains. It was a cozy nest hidden far away from anything that could harm it. She had a nice family of three little babies and took good care of them.

When their feathers began to grow, she knew that the day would soon come when they would have to leave the nest and learn to fly by themselves. They would have to find their own food. They would have to make their nests to raise their own families. So from time to time she warned them, "Be prepared. The day is coming for you to fly."

But the baby sparrows were lazy. They didn't really care if they ever grew up. They said to each other, "Our mother brings us all we need to eat. Our nest is cozy. Why should we grow up? As soon as our feathers are large enough for us to get hold of with our beaks, when Mommy isn't looking, we'll pull them out. Then we can keep on living right here in our nice warm nest, and Mommy will keep bringing us food."

Their mother became concerned. Her children seemed strong and healthy. Their bodies were almost big enough for them to begin learning to fly. But they still had no feathers. She kept telling them, "Children, you'd better be prepared. The day is coming for you to fly."

Then the season of rains came to an end. The scorching sun burned down on the prairie grass day after day. Soon the grass became brown and brittle. One day hunters came. They wanted to drive out the animals which were hiding in the tall dry grass. To do this they set the grass on fire. The hot flames leaped upward toward the sky and sped toward the tree. The mother bird became hotter and hotter. Soon she could stay there no longer. She spread out her wings and fluttered above the nest. She was sure it would do no good to tell her baby birds once again, but she cried out, "The day has come! Fly! Fly!" Then she lifted herself up into the sky to safety.

The baby birds were still throwing their bare arms around in the air when the fire reached them, but it did no good. They burned up. They hadn't listened, and so they weren't prepared.

Jesus said many times, "Watch now . . . the day of judgment is coming!" What day? The Bible says, "the day of judgment is coming, burning like a furnace. The proud and wicked will be burned up like straw; like a tree, they will be consumed—roots and all" (Malachi 4:1).

Are you playing when you should be listening? Are you careless when you should be learning?

Listen to the mother bird's warning: "You'd better be prepared; the day is coming."

We should turn our back to sin. We should learn to love Jesus and to walk with Him. Then, when the time comes, we'll be able to go to be with Jesus forever.

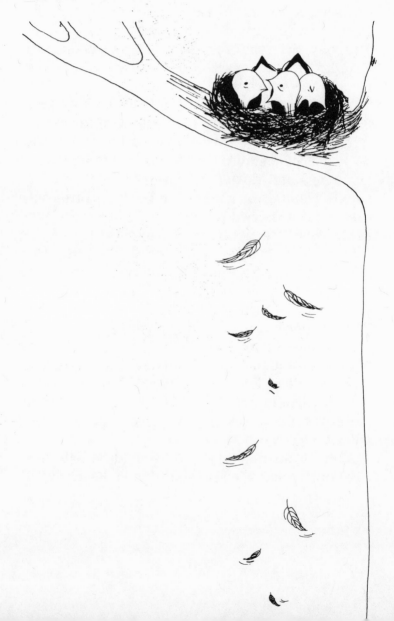

9

Miss Leopard's Strange Boyfriends

THERE ONCE was a leopard who thought he had the prettiest daughter in the forest. He didn't want his daughter to marry just anyone. How would he find a good husband for her?

"My daughter is valuable," he said to himself. "Whoever wants her should pay a high price for her. He should also be someone who is willing to work hard to provide for her. I know what I'll do. Whoever wants to marry her must build her a house in a half a day. Before the sun is straight up at dinner time, the house must be finished."

All the animals in the forest thought that was a high price for a wife. They asked each other, "Who can do that?" But they were all afraid of the leopard, because sometimes when something made him angry, he couldn't control his temper.

One day the deer decided that he would try to win the leopard's daughter for his wife. So he went to the leopard and asked for her.

The leopard said, "You know the price, don't you? You must build my daughter a house before the sun gets to the middle of the sky."

"Yes, I think I can do that," Mr. Deer said. "When shall I begin?"

"Tomorrow morning."

The next morning bright and early Mr. Deer was at the leopard's door. Mr. Leopard showed him where to build the house. Mr. Deer raced off to the forest for some sticks. He worked as fast as he could, running back and forth to the forest and pounding sticks into the ground to make walls. But his antlers kept getting tangled in the tree branches, and because his mouth was small, he could carry only one stick at a time. Meanwhile the sun kept rising higher and higher. When noontime came the deer had only two walls built.

Mr. Leopard shook his head and said, "I'm sorry, but you can't have my daughter for your wife."

After some days Mr. Elephant decided that he would try to marry Miss Leopard. He went to see her father. Mr. Leopard told him to return the next day.

Early the next morning Mr. Elephant was at Mr. Leopard's house. After he was shown where to build the house, he lumbered off to the forest for some sticks. Now the elephant is big and can carry many sticks at a time, but he can't move as fast as the deer; neither can his tiny eyes see as well. But he worked as fast as he could. By noon he was tired and sweaty and panting, but he had only built three walls.

Mr. Leopard shook his head and said, "I'm sorry, but you can't have her."

One day Mr. Crocodile decided to see if he could build a house for the leopard's daughter. He made a date when he was to begin. When the day arrived Mr. Crocodile was there before the sun came up. He worked as hard and fast as he could. He could carry lots of sticks at once in his big mouth. But a crocodile's skin becomes hard and cracks if it gets dry. So when the sun became hot he had to go back down to the river every once in awhile and make himself wet again. This took more time than he thought it would. By noontime Mr. Crocodile had four walls about finished, but he hadn't even started on the roof.

For many days the animals talked about the hard problem of trying to win Mr. Leopard's daughter. If fast Mr. Deer and strong Mr. Elephant and big-mouthed Mr. Crocodile were not able to build a house by noon, who could? They decided that Mr. Leopard would have to lower his price or no one would ever marry his daughter.

One day when Mr. Leopard was sleeping under a tree in his yard, he heard a little squeaky voice call.

"Excuse me, Mr. Leopard."

The leopard looked around, but he could see no one. He heard the voice again.

"Mr. Leopard."

This time he spied Mr. Fieldmouse at the edge of the clearing.

"What do you want?" he roared.

Mr. Fieldmouse trembled. Mr. Leopard's mouth was so big he could gobble a little mouse without even tasting him.

"I want to marry your daughter," the fieldmouse said.

"You want to marry my daughter?" Mr. Leopard opened his big mouth and roared with laughter. "Ha, ha, ha. You could never build her a house in half a day."

The frightened little mouse acted brave and asked, "But can't I try like everyone else?"

"All right, you may try. But neither the deer, the elephant, nor the crocodile was able to do it, and you are much smaller than they."

"I know. What day shall I come?"

"Come next Thursday," said Mr. Leopard.

Mr. Fieldmouse hurried off to the forest. He called together his whole tribe of fieldmice. He said to them.

"Next Thursday morning I am to build the leopard's daughter a house. If I get her for my wife, think what honor that will bring to the whole mouse tribe! None of the animals would ever again dare say that we are worthless little things. So I want all of you to help me."

"But what can we do?" they all asked.

"You know that cleared-out place in the forest where the leopard's house is? Thursday morning all of you come with sticks and hide in the forest on the edge of the clearing. You know that other animals never pay attention to us. They don't recognize one fieldmouse from another. I will run out and put my stick in place and run back into the forest again; then each of you will take his turn until we have the house finished."

The following Thursday morning all the mice were waiting there at the forest's edge with their sticks. Mr. Fieldmouse came to Mr. Leopard and said, "I'm here now; may I start?"

"Yes, go ahead. Let's see what a little mouse can do."

Then the mouse ran for his stick. He popped out into the clearing, put it into the ground, and ran back into the forest. Then another mouse popped out and in; then another, and another. The leopard watched in amazement. He could hardly believe his eyes. Never had he seen an animal of the forest work so hard. The little mouse never seemed to get tired either. He never stopped to rest until the house was done, and the sun hadn't quite reached the middle of the sky. Mr. Leopard had to keep his word. Mr. Fieldmouse took the leopard's daughter home to be his wife.

Some work we have to do will never get done if each of us insists on doing it all alone in his own way. If we love each other as the Bible says, we'll help each other. When we are willing to work hard together, we'll be able to get so much work done everybody will be surprised and ask, "How can they do it? We can't believe it."

10

The Braggy Crocodile

THREE MONKEYS loved to play in the trees of the forest, but they especially liked to play in the big tree that hung over the river. Beneath the tree was a nice sandbank where Mr. Crocodile liked to sun himself and sleep. One day when he was having a warm snooze, the monkeys came to play.

They were having fun chasing each other among the branches and chattering when their noise woke Mr. Crocodile from his nap. He squinted his little beady green eyes and growled loudly at them, "What are you doing here? Don't you know this is my nap time, and this is my place to sleep?"

"Who said this is your place? We can play here if we want to," taunted the monkeys.

"I'm chief of the river. Now beat it."

"Who said you're chief of the river?" they asked.

"Everybody knows it," roared the crocodile. "Now go away."

"Did you ever prove that you are chief of the river?" the monkeys chided. "We won't go away until you prove it."

"All right. How do you want me to prove that I'm chief of the river?"

"Why don't we have a tug-of-war?"

"Me have a tug-of-war with you little monkeys? Don't be ridiculous."

"We'll just keep on playing here then."

"All right. We'll have a tug-of-war. I'll pull you clear into the middle of the river so that you'll never bother me again. When will we do it?"

"Let's have it day after tomorrow."

With that the monkeys scampered off into the forest. Two of them started tying vines together to make two long pulling ropes. The third one went to look for Mr. Elephant. When he found him he said, "Mr. Elephant, you know how Mr. Crocodile is al-

ways bragging that he is chief of the river. We want to show him he isn't. Will you help us?"

"I don't like his growling and bossing either," said Mr. Elephant. "What can I do?"

The monkey ran up Mr. Elephant's trunk and whispered into his ear. "Ssssss." Mr. Elephant chuckled to himself and nodded that he understood.

By the next day all the forest animals had heard that there was going to be a tug-of-war between the monkeys and the crocodile. They all came to watch. Mr. Lion was chosen to be the referee. One monkey took a long rope and tied one end of it to Mr. Crocodile's front paw. Then he unrolled it into the forest where no one could see, to where Mr. Elephant was standing. There he tied one end to

Mr. Elephant's back leg. The other rope he tied to Mr. Elephant's trunk. Then the monkey brought the end of it out of the forest onto the plain where all their friends could see. There the monkeys took hold of it.

Mr. Lion was to be judge. "Everybody ready?" roared Mr. Lion.

"Ready!" shouted the monkeys.

"Ready," growled Mr. Cocodile.

"On your marks. Get set. PULL!"

The three little monkeys pulled for all they were worth. Mr. Crocodile pulled too. But the harder he pulled, the more he seemed to be slipping out of the water. Surely he was stronger than those monkeys. But he just kept slipping out of the water. Bit by bit, his tummy came out of the water, followed by his back legs. What was wrong? He grabbed for a rock and then for a tree root. But he kept slipping out of the river toward the forest. Soon only the tip of his tail was left in the water.

"Hurray!" shouted all the animals. "The monkeys are chief of the river!"

Mr. Crocodile was so embarrassed that he slipped the rope from his foot and slid back into the river and hasn't come back to bother anybody since.

The Bible says, "Pride goes before destruction and a haughtiness before a fall" (Proverbs 16:18). It's not nice to be bossy and braggy and act like you know everything, like Mr. Crocodile. If you do, you'd better be careful, because some little monkey may come along and make a fool out of you.

11

The Mole Who Wanted to Swim Before Dinner

DEEP in the forest lived a fox and a mole who were coming to be good friends. To strengthen their friendship, they decided to begin eating together.

The fox said, "I can always catch a chicken."

The mole said, "I know where I can get flour for mush. I've watched women make grain into flour with their pounding tools at the edge of the village."

So they agreed to eat their first meal together the afternoon of the next day.

In the morning the fox sneaked into the village and caught a chicken. The mole took a sack and burrowed a long tunnel under the ground to the flour-pounding place. He burrowed right through the bottom of a basket of flour. He filled his sack, and carried it back to his house. There he found the fox waiting with a chicken. They put the meat on the fire and cooked the flour to make mush. They ate together, and then went to sleep.

The next morning the fox said again, "I'm going to catch a chicken."

The mole said, "I'm going for flour."

But the mole had another idea too. As soon as the fox left, the mole went to the river nearby. Just beneath the water's edge he burrowed a hole in the riverbank all the way back inside his hut. He covered the hole with a basket. Then he went for flour.

When the mole returned home with the flour he found the fox waiting with a chicken. They prepared the meal. Then the mole said to the fox, "Oh, Friend Fox, let's first go to the river and swim. Then we'll come and eat and sleep well."

The fox thought it sounded like a good idea; so he said, "Very well, let's go."

They went down the path to the river. At the river the fox jumped in, swam across the river and back again, then got out.

The mole said to him, "When I get into the water, you won't see me so soon. I like to stay under for a long time."

Then the mole dived in, swam to the tunnel, ran through it all the way to his house, ate all the food, and then returned. When he came up out of the water, he took a big breath of fresh air, and said, "Let's go now."

The fox said, "My, you sure can stay under a long time."

The mole said, "Yes, I like water. It's my custom to swim this way."

When they arrived at the house, they found all the food gone.

"Who ate all the food?" asked the fox.

"We both went swimming. How could I know?"

answered the mole. They stared at each other in silence, and soon they went to bed. But the fox was still hungry.

The next day they got meat and flour and fixed their food again. The mole said, "Let's go swimming. I enjoy it so much."

"I don't care to go. Let's eat first," answered the fox.

The mole said, "Oh, but we won't stay long. We'll swim only a short time."

Finally the fox gave in. So they hurried down the path to the river. The mole jumped in, slipped into his tunnel, went to his house, ate all the food, and returned. When they came back to the house and saw that the food was gone again, the fox said, "See. It happened again. That's why I said, 'Let's eat first.' " That night the fox went to bed terribly hungry.

The next morning the fox went earlier for the chicken and the mole went for flour. The fox

returned to the house before the mole did. He went to the river to see what he could find. He jumped into the water where the mole always jumped in. Sure enough he found the tunnel that led toward the house. When the fox saw it he said to himself, "Why, that fellow has an underground path to his house. The mole is tricking me." He quickly built a trap in the mouth of the tunnel. Then he went back to cook the chicken.

After they had cooked the food the mole again said, "Now let's go for a swim."

"Are you sure you want to go swimming again today?" asked the fox.

"Oh yes, it's a custom I enjoy very much." So they went to the river.

The mole jumped into the river. The fox watched and waited for a long, long time. Finally he jumped in to look for the mole. He found him dead, caught in the trap. So the fox went back to the mole's house and took his time eating the whole meal by himself.

Sometimes we can fool our friends or our parents like the mole did the fox. But we can't fool them all the time. After a while we'll get caught. Sometimes we even think we are fooling God. But we aren't. He knows everything.

In the Bible we read, "You may be sure that your sins will catch up with you," and "For the wages of sin is death" (Numbers 32:23; Romans 6:23). When we try to fool God by sinning and think He doesn't know, we are only fooling ourselves. Unless we are sorry and ask Jesus to forgive us, someday we'll have to pay for our sin.

12

The Hunter Whose Stomach Was Too Big

THERE was a man who made his living by hunting. It was the only kind of work he could do well. He was very skillful. Every day he brought meat from the forest. Some he, his wife, and children ate. Other meat he sold to buy them clothing. They had all they needed.

Once he took his bow and arrows and spent all day in the forest. He didn't get anything. Tired and discouraged, he went on his way home. Just as he was leaving the forest, he found a prairie tree covered with caterpillars.

"What good luck!" he said. "We haven't had any of these to eat with our mush for a whole year." He began stripping the caterpillars off the branches and putting them into his hunting bag.

Pretty soon a little wren started darting around in the limbs and warning, "Share what you find, or you'll lose what you have."

"Foolish wren," he thought. "Me and my family hungry as we are, and a tree full of caterpillars. Who is there to share with?"

He stuffed his hunting bag full, took it home, and he and his family feasted on caterpillars and mush.

The hunter slept so well that night that he didn't want to go hunting the next morning. "Surely I can have one day of vacation," he told himself. "I'll rest this morning. After dinner I'll go to the tree again and bring caterpillars home in time for supper."

When he got to the tree, the caterpillars were still there; and so was the wren. When the hunter began stripping caterpillars off more of the branches, the wren became very excited. He sang his warning song over and over again as he darted around on the branches: "Share what you find, or you'll lose what you have!"

The hunter was too greedy to share something so good with someone he couldn't see. He kept on working hard to fill his bag. Suddenly a branch near him began wriggling. Then an end of it raised and darted out and bit him on the elbow. It was a snake who also liked to feast on caterpillars. The wren stopped singing.

The hunter cried out in pain. He ran home as fast as he could go. His wife put medicine onto the bite and helped him to bed. The hunter didn't die, but his elbow became paralyzed so that it could never pull his hunting bow again.

God has a rule that people who are greedy will end up poor, and people who share what they have will be given more. If I have plenty of something and I refuse to share with someone in need, it just shows that I do not have God's love in my heart.

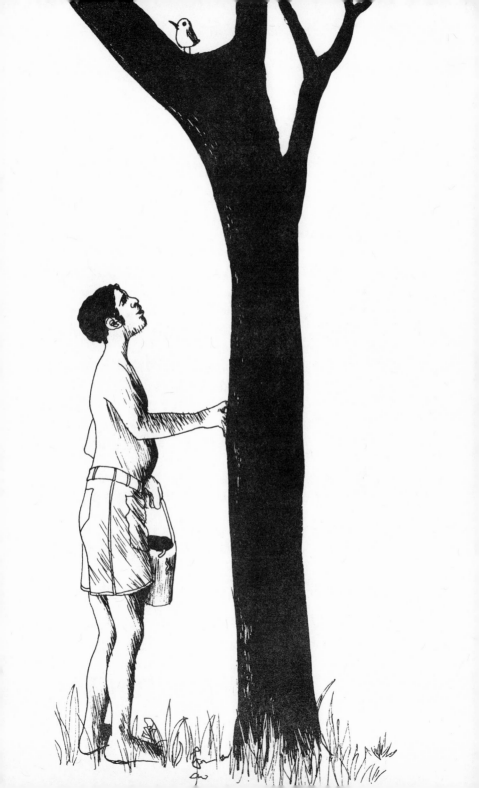

13

Who Is Big Enough to Rescue a Lion?

ONE DAY a hungry lion was walking through the forest hunting for something to eat. When he stepped on a leaf, a tiny mouse jumped out from under it. The lion slammed his paw to the ground and caught the mouse by its tail.

"Please, Mr. Lion, don't eat me," pleaded the mouse. "Remember that kindness brings more kindness. If you let me go, the day may come when I will more than repay you. Besides, why should the King of the Forest want to eat a tiny thing like me?"

The lion scoffed at the thought that the mouse might ever do anything kind for him. But he was flattered that the mouse called him "King of the Forest." And it was true that even if he should eat the mouse, he would still be just as hungry. He decided there was no good reason for killing a helpless little animal, so he lifted his paw, and the mouse scampered away.

Time passed. One day the mouse was out hunting seeds to eat when he heard the most terrible noise.

It sounded like some big animal was roaring and snarling and moaning all at once. The mouse shivered with fear, but he had to find out what it was. Carefully he made his way along a hidden path under the brush toward the noise and peered out from under a leaf. Mr. Lion was caught in a hunter's net. Fighting with his four legs had just gotten him tangled up worse.

"Just a minute, sir. I'll help you!" cried the mouse.

Mr. Lion was throwing himself around and making such a ruckus that he never even heard the mouse. But the more he fought, the tighter the net bound him. He was terribly angry and dreadfully afraid. He knew that soon the hunter would be coming to check his net trap, and that would mean death. He kept fighting until he became weary and began to lose hope that he would ever be free again.

Then all of a sudden he felt a net rope snap loose; after a while another one snapped loose. He began squinting his eyes and turning his head this way and that trying to see who was rescuing him. Finally he saw the tiny mouse busy chewing through the net ropes.

When the work was all done, you can be sure that there was no one in all the world happier than Mr. Lion.

"Mr. Mouse," he said, "I want you to tell all your family and relatives that I'll never bother a member of the mouse tribe again."

Sometimes we don't want to be kind. We're too tired, or we don't have time, or we have ugly feelings in our hearts. But we should do our best to show kindness every time we can.

God promises us that every kind thing we do today, even if it seems very little, will someday be more than repaid. Jesus said that even if we give somebody a drink of cool water, we'll get our reward.

14

The Powerful Little Fly

THE FLY had just finished feasting on the carcass of a millipede. His tummy felt so full and good he wanted to find someone to tease. Suddenly he spied Mr. Hippopotamus basking on a sunny sandbank. He buzzed past the lazy hippo's head, tickled his ear, and said, "Do you know I'm stronger than you are?"

The sleepy hippo answered, "Don't be ridiculous. Go away and leave me alone."

"If you don't believe it," teased the fly, "just wait around awhile and you'll see."

He buzzed into the hippo's ear. He tickled his nostrils. The hippo twitched his ears, tossed his head, sneezed, and finally got up and lumbered lazily off into the water where the fly couldn't bother him anymore.

"See. What did I tell you?" boasted the little fly, as he circled over the hippo a last time and headed back toward the forest. He was so happy he'd been born a strong little fly, and not a lazy hippo. All of a sudden BANG! He ran into a wall he couldn't see. It was springy and sticky. His feet got caught in it. He tried every way to get unstuck but couldn't. It was a spider's web.

Sometimes we feel quite proud of ourselves and boast about the big things we can do and the wonderful plans we have. Yet we never know what lies ahead for us. The Bible says, "Don't brag about your plans for tomorrow—wait and see what happens" (Proverbs 27:1).

By ourselves we have nothing to brag about. Every day of our life is a gift from God.

15

People Don't Have Any Ears

ONCE UPON A TIME there was an old lion who was not able to hunt as he once had. He noticed that people have large bodies and run slowly. So he started catching people.

Many people lived in the village of Tshiawa. One day the lion caught someone in the village down the path from them. The next morning the village chief climbed up onto his hut roof and cried out, "Listen, my people. A bad lion is in our forest. Today no one will go to the stream or to the field. Everyone must stay in the village. Do you hear?"

Everyone listened carefully. They all obeyed except one woman, Meta.

Her water gourds were empty. She didn't see how she could do without water that day. How would she cook? How would she bathe her baby? She must have water. She would make a quick trip. It wasn't far. She put her empty gourds into her long narrow carrying basket, balanced the basket on her head, and went to the stream.

Everything seemed to be all right. She arrived at

the stream, walked into the shallow water, and filled each of her gourds. She put them into her basket and was lifting it onto her head when SWISHHHHH, from the bushes the old lion leaped upon her and killed her. He was carrying her along the prairie path to his den when he met strong Mr. Leopard.

"Where are you going with all that good meat?" asked Mr. Leopard.

"I'm going to my den," answered the lion.

"Why don't you let me help you carry such a heavy load?"

"No, thank you. You needn't carry it for me," answered the lion. "But I must admit I am a bit tired. Would you watch it for me? That way I can go get a drink of water and rest in the shade a bit before continuing the long journey to my den. You won't eat it, will you?"

"Of course not. Would a child steal from a grandfather? I'll guard it well."

So off went the lion, leaving the leopard to guard.

The leopard waited a long time. The sun climbed higher and higher. It grew hotter and hotter. Meanwhile the leopard grew more and more hungry. Whenever he looked at the fresh meat before him, his mouth watered. How hungry he was! Finally he thought to himself, "I'll just eat one of her ears. The old lion would never know the difference." He ate one. After a bit he ate the other one.

Finally Mr. Lion came back. He looked at his catch. Then he looked at Mr. Leopard.

"Where are her ears?" he asked.

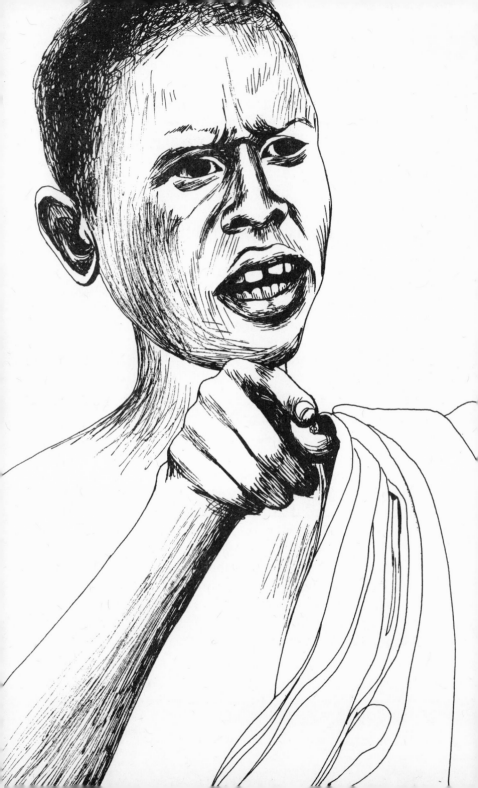

"Oh friend Lion, people don't have any ears."

"Oh yes they do; they *always* do. She had ears when I left her with you. What happened to them?"

"I'm sorry, Mr. Lion, but people don't have any ears. If you like, I will prove it to you."

"Then you'd better prove it," the lion growled.

"All right. This evening just as the sun is going to bed, meet me at the path-crossing near the village," invited the leopard.

That evening just as the sun was setting, the two animals met at the path-crossing. Then the leopard led the old lion through the tall grass to the edge of the village. There they waited quietly.

People in the village were stirring around frantically. No one could find Meta. She had evidently gone for water in spite of what the chief had said.

Soon the lion and leopard saw the chief of the village climb onto the top of his roof. Then they heard him cry out, "Listen to me, my people. This morning I told you there was a lion nearby. I told you not to go to the forest or the stream. Meta refused to listen to my words. She went anyway. Why don't you people obey me? Why don't you listen to me? You people don't have any ears."

The leopard turned to the old lion and said, "There, you heard what the man said. People don't have any ears."

Jesus said, "He who has ears to hear, let him hear" (Matthew 11:15, RSV). Do you have ears? Are you using them to listen to what Jesus says? Or do you turn them off when there's something you don't want to hear?

If we refuse to listen, then it's only our fault when something bad happens. Solomon the wise man said, "If you have good eyesight and good hearing, thank God who gave them to you" (Proverbs 20:12). Jesus wants us to use them for Him.

16

The Little Load That Was Too Big for an Elephant

BIG MR. ELEPHANT sat gloomily on a stump with his trunk propped over his shoulder. He was so lonely. No one wanted to be his friend—absolutely no one.

Mr. Canary heard about Mr. Elephant's sadness and decided to go comfort him. "I'll be your friend," he said.

The elephant was delighted. "Can you come to our house next week and eat a friendship feast with me? Then our friendship will last forever!"

The canary felt greatly honored. "Yes, I'll be happy to come," he said.

So the next week the canary went to the elephant's house. He sat and watched Mrs. Elephant finish the meal for them. She loaded the table down with far more then he could eat. He was so happy to have found such a generous friend. After the meal, Mr. Elephant loaded Mr. Canary's arms with many good things for his wife.

Mr. Canary took the good things home to his wife and told her what had happened. Mrs. Canary listened carefully. The longer he talked the more she frowned. When he finished the story, he asked, "Why are you frowning?"

She looked him straight in the eye and said, "Mr. Canary, when Mr. Elephant sends word that he's coming to our house for a feast in return for his good favor, just where do you think we'll find enough things to fill HIS big stomach? If you keep his friendship, he'll eat up everything we've got. Don't you understand? That's why other animals don't want to be his friend."

Mr. Canary hadn't thought about that. Why was his wife always thinking ahead of him? "W-e-l-l, when we hear he's coming, we'll figure out something," he replied weakly.

After some time Mr. Elephant sent a message that he was coming.

"All right, Mr. Canary, now what are you going to do?" asked Mrs. Canary.

On the day the elephant was to come, Mr. Canary said, "I've got it figured out. Pull out all my feathers and hold me in your arms. When Mr. Elephant arrives, tell him that I am away searching for the things we need for the feast, and that you are left to care for the new little baby."

Soon they heard the bushes cracking and the branches snapping. Mr. Elephant was coming. When he arrived at the canary hut, Mrs. Canary was seated by the fire holding her baby. "Why hello, Mr. Elephant," she said.

"Hello. Is your husband here?"

"No, he isn't," she replied. "Ever since he heard

that you were coming he has been away gathering the things we will need for the feast. I'm very lonesome because he has been away for a long time. This little baby has come since he left. I have no one to help me get food and firewood."

"Oh, I'm very sorry about that," replied the elephant sympathetically. "I'll be glad to help you until he returns. We're good friends. Please, I would like to take your baby home with me and watch him. I'll take good care of him until Mr. Canary returns. I'll be glad to send you some food as well."

Mrs. Canary didn't want to refuse and make Mr. Elephant feel badly. After all, their families had agreed to be friends. So she placed her baby into the elephant's care, "You take good care of him," she said. "He's the only child I have. I'll call you as soon as my husband comes back."

Mr. Elephant started home, his big trunk curled around the tiny bird. Because it was so small, the elephant had a difficult time carrying it. It made his journey slow and tiring. At the first river he decided to stop and bathe. Mr. Canary saw his chance, and quickly slipped into the forest and ran all the way home.

When Mr. Elephant finished his bath, he went to pick up the baby to be on his way. The baby wasn't there. He looked and looked, but he couldn't find it anywhere. "Now what must I do?" he thought. "It would be cruel to go on. I guess I must return and break the awful news to Mrs. Canary."

When Mr. Elephant came into the clearing Mrs.

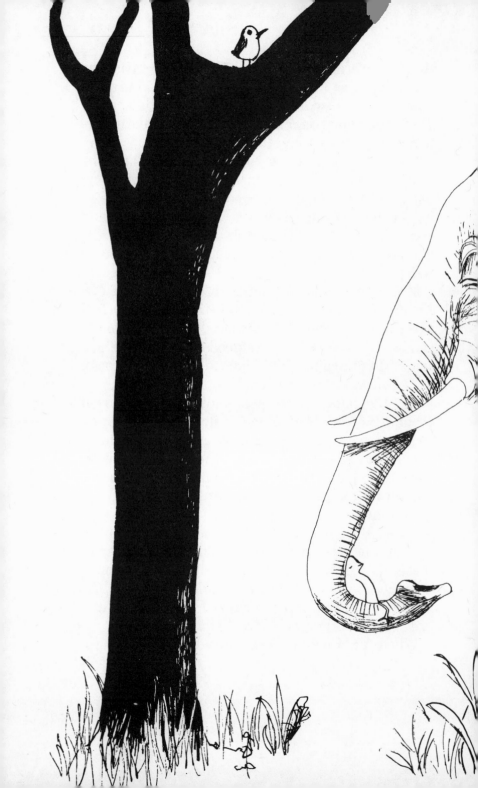

Canary was seated alone by the fire. "Oh, Mrs. Canary," he cried, "have you seen your baby?"

"Have *I* seen my baby? Don't you have him?"

Mr. Elephant sat down and tried to break the awful news. He explained how her baby had disappeared. Mrs. Canary was heartbroken. But through her tears, she found some comfort when Mr. Elephant assured her that he would hunt some more and surely find the baby.

But Mr. Elephant never did find the baby. And he never came back to see Mr. and Mrs. Canary again.

When we become Christians we agree to be friends with Christ. This is the most serious promise a person can ever make. If we really love the one we've pledged our friendship to, we won't try to play tricks on Him.

God wants us to do things which will make our friendship with Him stronger, like reading His Word, singing songs about Him, talking to Him in prayer, and telling others about Him. He wants us to do the things which will help our friendship last forever.

17

Can Puppies Stop Sniffing?

ONE DAY a puppy was sitting and thinking when a strange idea came to him. "Why is it that I'm always running helter-skelter with my nose up in the air sniffing for some new scent?" he asked himself. "None of my other animal friends acts this way. Is this something only our family does? I sure was unlucky to be born a dog and do such funny things."

He went and curled up under a tree to think about his problem. He was feeling more and more sorry for himself when along came Mr. Owl.

"Oh, Mr. Owl," cried the puppy. "Are you wise enough to break the curse I was born with? Why is it that I find myself running here and there with my nose tipped in the air hunting for a scent?"

Mr. Owl replied, "If I tell you how to break the curse of this habit you have, will you follow all my directions carefully?"

"Oh, I will keep whatever rules you make for me as long as I live, if only they will help me be like other animals," promised the puppy.

"If you strictly obey me," the wise owl said, "you will become like other animals. There is just one rule: if you smell any unusual scent, *don't* lift your nose, and *don't* run to see what it is without my permission. Do you understand?"

"Oh yes, Mr. Owl," replied the puppy.

The owl wanted to see how sincere the puppy was in his promise. So he went behind the house and borrowed a few tail feathers from Friend Rooster. Then he placed them in a hole in the ground and set them on fire.

The puppy smelled the strange odor. He dashed around the house sniffing the air, and ran squarely into Mr. Owl.

"My friend, aren't you ashamed of yourself?" the

wise owl chided. "I told you that when you smelled a scent, you were not to follow it without my permission. But you weren't able to keep that simple rule. It looks as though you will never be able to break the curse you were born with."

And so, to this very day, dogs still run around helter-skelter sniffing the air.

We, like the puppy, were born with a curse. The curse is sin. People naturally love to sin. In spite of all the promises we make to be good, we always find ourselves going back to sin. The only way we can free ourselves from this curse is to become born all over again. God will make us into new persons. He will help us live as we should.

Jesus said that there is no way for a person to enter the kingdom of heaven except to be born again and made into a new person (John 3:3).

Have you asked Jesus to live in your heart? Or are you like the puppy—still trying to find your own way to break the curse you were born with?

18

The Little Goat Who Couldn't See Enough

THE LITTLE goat and the little jackal were very good friends. Each day they played together in the tall grass around the edge of the village. They had many happy times together.

One morning when they came to their place of playing, the little jackal was all excited. "Do you know what?" he said. "I saw a leopard last night. He was real big."

"What did he look like?" the goat asked.

"He's big and has lots of spots on him."

"I want to see a big, live leopard," the little goat begged.

"Oh no. He's a dangerous fellow. I can't let you see him," answered the jackal.

"But I want to see him," the goat whined.

"No, no. I can't let you see him. He's too dangerous."

For many days they talked about the leopard, and for many days the little goat begged to see it. Finally one day the jackal said, "All right. Meet me here when the sun is this low." He pointed with his hand to a five-o-clock sun. "I'll show you the leopard."

That evening when the sun was getting low, the little goat ran out to the high grass to meet his friend. The jackal took the goat behind a big rock and left him there. After a while the goat heard a noise. He peeked around the rock, but all he could see was the tip of the tail of the leopard as he went through the grass.

The next morning when the two came to play the jackal asked the goat if he had seen the leopard.

"All I saw was the tip of his tail. I want to see his eyes," answered the goat.

"Oh no," replied the jackal. "I can't let you see his eyes. He's a bad fellow."

"But I want to see him."

Finally after some days the jackal got tired of the goat's begging and agreed to take him out to see the leopard again. This time the jackal took the goat a little closer to the leopard's path. Again he left the goat by himself. Soon the little goat heard the noise of the leopard coming. This time he saw the side of the leopard go by. But he still was not satisfied.

He told his friend, "I want to see his eyes. I want to look into his eyes."

The little jackal said, "No, never. He's much too dangerous. I could never let you do that."

Finally after the goat begged a long time the jackal sighed and took the goat to where he could see the leopard. He put the little goat right on the path where the leopard would pass that night. The little jackal went away quickly, leaving the goat by himself.

This time the little goat was a bit afraid. He wasn't sure what might happen. Pretty soon it was dark. It was not long until he heard a noise on the path. Sure enough, the leopard was coming. What would he do? This evening the leopard was very hungry. When he saw the little goat, they looked right into each other's eyes. Then the leopard pounced upon the goat and ate him up.

It isn't always good to insist on seeing things others tell us are not good for us. If the little goat had not insisted on seeing something that was not good for him, he would have been better off.

Sometimes when we insist on doing things which aren't good for us, we only hurt ourselves. If we insist on playing with sin, sooner or later we'll get caught.

The Bible says, "Temptation is the pull of man's own evil thoughts and wishes. These evil thoughts lead to evil actions and afterwards to the death penalty from God" (James 1:14, 15).

19

What Do You Need to Be a Chief?

THE GREAT CHIEF of a tribal kingdom had only one son. Because he had only one son, it was very important that he train him well. Someday this boy would take his place. If he trained him poorly and the boy was not a good chief, his people would not remember him kindly. If the boy ruled well, the people would have happy memories of his father.

So all the years while the boy was growing up, his father tried to prepare him for his future. Finally the day came for the chief to test his son, as was the custom.

He took his bag of magic medicines, a hoe, and his son, and went on a journey into the forest. The father and the boy walked down the trail together until they reached the thick dark center of the jungle. There they came to a clearing. In the center of the clearing the father took the hoe and dug a large circle in the ground. He put the boy in the center of it. Then he said, "My child, no matter what happens, you must not leave this circle until I come for you again. Do you understand?"

"Yes, I understand," answered the boy. The father left the clearing and hid in the forest nearby to watch.

The boy sat down on the ground to wait. He felt terribly alone and afraid. He wondered what had happened to his father. Soon he heard a rustling sound in the underbrush. He strained his ears to hear where it was coming from. Then he saw something coming toward him. It was a big black snake!

The boy jumped up, ready to run. Then he remembered the words of his father: "My child, you must not leave this circle until I come for you again." He could not disobey his father; so he sat down again.

The snake came closer and closer until it reached the edge of the circle. It fastened its beady eyes on the boy, shifting its head slowly from side to side as if it were going to strike him. Then something seemed to change its mind, and it slowly turned and went away.

The boy sat in the quietness for what seemed like a long time. Then he was terrified by the roar of a lion. It roared again so fiercely that it shook the tree branches. Chills of fear raced down the boy's backbone. What would he do if the lion found him? Should he run away?

Then the boy saw the lion's flaming eyes peer at him from under the bushes. Suddenly the lion gave a great leap toward him, and landed on the very edge of the circle. He prowled around its edge

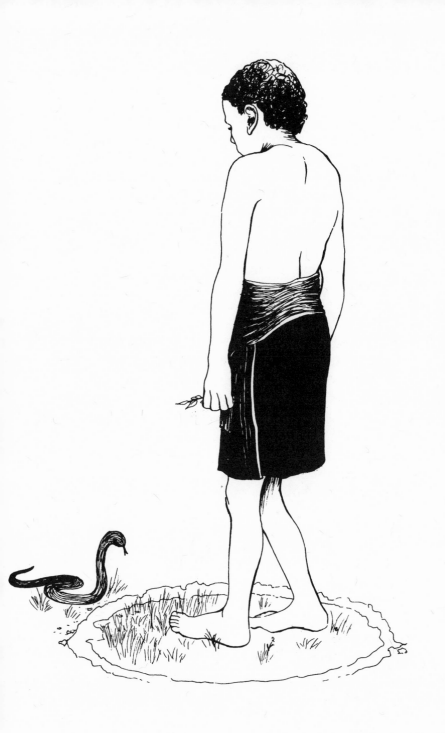

growling. The boy turned and turned with the lion, keeping his eyes on it all the time. Finally the lion gave a great roar of anger, turned, and went back into the forest.

The sun was getting low in the sky; the jungle was becoming dark. Still the father had not come back. The boy was lonesome, and hungry, and terribly afraid. Had his father forgotten him? Maybe he would never return.

Then the boy smelled something strange. He heard dry branches crackling. He turned to look, and sure enough, he saw the flames of a forest fire. The flames came closer and closer. They jumped high into the treetops and heaved great billows of black smoke into the sky. Should he run? No, he would stay even if he burned up.

The flames came closer and closer until the fire was so hot he could hardly breathe. But when the flames reached the edge of the circle, they began to die down, until finally they went out, leaving the ground all around him black and smoking.

Then from the edge of the jungle came his father. How happy the boy was to see him! The father gathered the boy into his arms and said, "Son, you are a very brave and obedient boy. I sent the snake and the lion and the fire. I wanted to try you. You have proven yourself. You will become a worthy chief when I die. Let us return to the village."

The young boy was now sure that if he kept on obeying and trusting his father, everything would come out all right.

Sometimes we may not understand the hard

things which happen to us in life. Sometimes we are afraid and wonder if our heavenly Father really cares for us. But we must remember that He is always watching us. Even when we can't understand everything, He wants us to trust and to obey Him. This way He will be pleased with us and happy to have us as His children.

20

The Crocodile Who Needed
a True Friend

MR. CROCODILE, his wife, and four small children lived happily in their stick-and-leaf house by the side of the stream. One day Mrs. Crocodile became very ill. Before the doctor could be reached, she died.

Mr. Crocodile was very sad. He decided that it would be too lonesome to live alone with his children, and so he decided to search for a faithful friend with whom he could live. He wanted someone to help him with all the problems of raising his family. After a long slow journey with the children he arrived at the home of Friend Wolf.

When Mr. Wolf heard of the death of Mrs. Crocodile, he was heartbroken, and cried many big tears. "What can I do to help?" he asked sorrowfully.

"I would appreciate it very much," replied Mr. Crocodile, "if you would help me find a palm tree with a bunch of ripe nuts. The children are so hungry."

Mr. Wolf kindly agreed to help him, and soon

Daddy Crocodile was trying to climb the palm tree with his knife. Now a knife is an awkward thing for a crocodile to hold onto, especially while climbing a tree, for crocodiles do not ordinarily climb trees, you know. After working hard he was high on the trunk, almost to the first set of branches where the nuts were clustered between the branch and the trunk. Suddenly he lost his grip, fell tumbling head over tail, and hit the ground kerrooomp! There he lay, silent and still.

"Oh Daddy! Daddy!" the children cried as they gathered around him.

The wolf picked up Mr. Crocodile's front paw and felt for his pulse. Then, shaking his head sadly, he said, "He's dead. What a shame. Oh, Wife, bring me a sharp knife. Let me skin this carcass and make myself a fine crocodile-skin carrying-bag."

"Skin me!" cried the crocodile as he rolled over and jumped to his feet. "I'm searching for a friend whom I can love and trust and with whom I can live forever. But it isn't you, traitor!" And with that he gathered his children into his arms and disappeared into the forest.

"I never did feel that Mr. Wolf was a true friend," grumbled Mr. Crocodile. "I'll visit Mr. Antelope. He has always been more kindly and understanding."

Mr. Antelope listened to the crocodile tell about the death of his wife. Then he embraced Mr. Crocodile for a long time, cried with him, and whispered words of comfort into his ear.

"My dear friend," the antelope said, "if there is anything I can do. . . ."

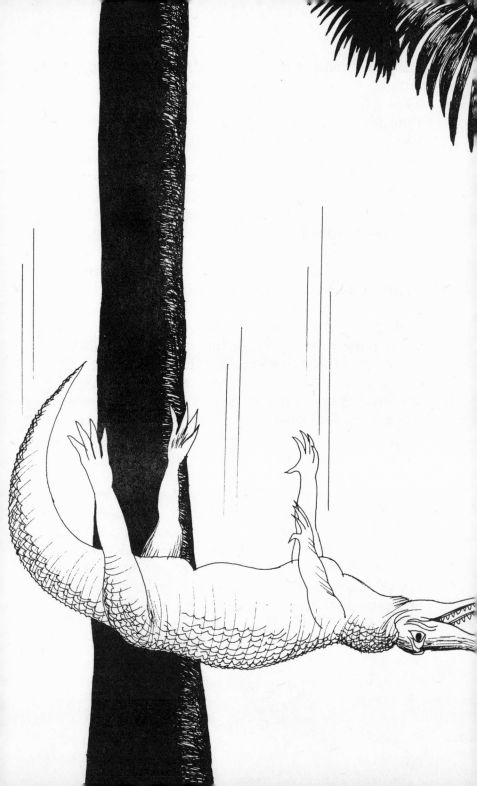

"If you'll just help me find a bunch of palm nuts—my children are so hungry," replied the crocodile.

Mr. Antelope was very helpful, and found a tree. Soon Daddy Crocodile was slowly making his way up the trunk with the knife in his hand. When he had almost reached the nuts, his hind foot slipped, and he came tumbling to the ground. The children gathered around him crying, "Oh Daddy, Daddy!"

"Well, I do believe he is dead," exclaimed the antelope. "What a misfortune. Wife, come. Shall we call our friends for the funeral? But what a pity to bury this whole carcass when we might use a bit of his beautiful skin to make you a purse and me a pair of shoes."

"My beautiful skin for a purse and shoes?" cried Mr. Crocodile. "I'm looking for a friend whom I can love and trust and with whom I can live forever. But it isn't you, traitor!" And once again he gathered his children into his arms and returned into the forest to continue his journey.

"How disappointing," he thought. "I'll go see Friend Armadillo. It seems I have more in common with him than I do with these hairy animals anyhow."

Mr. Armadillo greeted his old friend the crocodile with open arms. When he heard the news of Mrs. Crocodile's death he was very sad. When he knew Mr. Crocodile wanted palm nuts, he worked hard to find a tree; he liked to eat palm nuts himself.

Again Mr. Crocodile struggled up the trunk until

he almost reached the first set of branches. And what do you think happened? That's right. And once again the children gathered weeping around his silent body.

"Oh, wife," called Mr. Armadillo as he stooped to embrace his old friend. "Mr. Crocodile fell from the tree and is unconscious. Bring water quickly and a big leaf to fan him. We must do all we can to help him."

Mr. Crocodile listened carefully to hear if Mr. Armadillo said anything about his beautiful skin. But the armadillo showed him only kindness until he got better. Then he took hold of Mr. Armadillo's hand, shook it, and said, "I've been searching for a friend whom I can love and trust and with whom I can live forever. I'm not looking any more. Your kindness shows me that my search is ended."

Jesus is a true Friend, a Friend every one of us can trust no matter what happens. To prove that He can be trusted, He gave His life to save us from our sins. The Bible says, "When we were utterly helpless with no way of escape, Christ came at just the right time and died for us sinners who had no use for him. Even if we were good, we really wouldn't expect anyone to die for us, though of course, that might be barely possible. But God showed his great love for us by sending Christ to die for us while we were still sinners" (Romans 5:6-8). Where else can you find a friend as true as that?

21

The Pigs Who Despised Their Watchman

THE WILD PIGS lived in a clearing in the center of the forest. Every day they went to a big tree in the forest to eat nuts. They liked the nuts very much. Each evening they came home to their clearing.

Near the forest lived a hunter. Each day he went hunting. He would kill something and bring it to his house and dress it. Then he would tell his children to carry it into the kitchen to cook it. He never failed to bring something home.

One day his children asked him, "Father, you bring us the meat of all kinds of animals except wild pig. Why don't you bring us a pig?"

"I don't know why, but I can't catch them. Every time I come near to where they feed on nuts in the forest, they run away and I can't shoot them," answered the hunter.

One day when the wild pigs and their chief came home from the nut tree, they went through the village of the antelope and heard mourning. They asked the antelope, "Who died?"

"The hunter killed one of our relatives today," he replied.

As they went home they began boasting to their chief, "The hunter kills all the other animals, but he never gets us."

"You aren't safe because of your cleverness," the chief answered them. "You're safe because of a watchman."

The pigs didn't understand, and soon they forgot about it.

On their way home the next day the pigs passed through the village of the monkeys and found them mourning. When the pigs asked what had happened, they received the same answer: the hunter had killed a monkey.

On another day when they passed through the village of the elephants, there was great mourning. The pigs inquired again, "What happened?"

The elephants replied, "The hunter killed one of our friends in the forest."

On the way home the pigs began talking. "Those animals sure must be stupid! Always getting killed by the hunter."

But their chief warned them, "You should not boast. Didn't I tell you that you eat nuts safely because of a watchman?"

The pigs talked it over between themselves and decided, "No, having a watchman has nothing to do with our getting nuts."

One morning the chief of the wild pigs told the others, "I am sick. I can't go with you to get nuts today. You'd better stay at home."

But the pigs said, "We know how to get there!" and they went anyway. They arrived at the tree and found many nuts on the ground. They happily ate whatever they saw before their eyes, and didn't look up to see if anyone was near. They just kept eating and eating.

Suddenly there was a loud BANG! BANG! BANG! Two pigs fell dead. Three others were wounded. The rest ran for home as fast as their legs could carry them. When they came close to their village they began to wail and mourn. When they arrived the chief asked them, "What happened?"

They answered. "The hunter came. He killed two of us and wounded some others." Then they sat on the ground rocking back and forth, weeping and wailing.

The chief said, "Tomorrow I will go with you and you will see that you are safe to eat nuts because of a watchman."

The next day they were scared, but they went to eat nuts. The chief did what he had always done. Instead of eating, he walked around the herd, sniffing the air and looking in all directions. Suddenly he spotted leaves moving in the distance. He sniffed real hard. Yes, that was the hunter. He gave a little warning "oink," and before the pigs even thought about why, they were running.

This happened for five days. The hunter killed none. On the evening of the fifth day the chief called the pigs together and asked them, "Are you eating nuts?"

"Yes."

"Are you getting killed?"

"No."

"How do you know when to run from the hunter?" he asked.

"Because you warn us 'Oink'," they said.

"Don't you see that you eat nuts safely because of a watchman?"

Too often we are like those little pigs, gobbling up all the good things of life day after day, never stopping to think that we owe anybody anything. We have healthy bodies. We have food and a warm place to live. We enjoy these good things because Someone is watching over us.

The Bible says that a man can receive nothing except it be given him from heaven (John 3:27). Jesus is the giver of all good things. We must never be selfish and proud and boast of our cleverness. We have all the good things we enjoy because of Jesus, our Shepherd-watchman.

Eudene Keidel is a graduate of Fort Wayne Bible College, Fort Wayne, Indiana, and of Mennonite School of Nursing, Bloomington, Illinois.

She and her husband, Levi, have served under the Africa Inter-Mennonite Mission in Zaire since 1951 in a variety of medical and teaching ministries. They are the parents of four grown children.

A native of Flanagan, Illinois, Mrs. Keidel is a member of Maplewood Mennonite Church, Fort Wayne, Indiana.